CW00818985

How Many Freemasons Does it Take to Change a Light Bulb?

Martin Faulks

Lewis Masonic

First published 2005

ISBN 0 85318 243 4

Published by Lewis Masonic

an imprint of Ian Allan Publishing Ltd, Hersham, Surrey KT12 4RG.
Printed in England by Ian Allan Printing Ltd, Hersham, Surrey
KT12 4RG.

Front cover: Cover artwork supplied courtesy of Rowan Lee-Foyster.

Q: How many
    Freemasons
does it take to
   change
a light bulb?

   A: It's a secret.

Q: How many Freemasons does it take to change a light bulb?

A: Three. One to screw it in, one to read the minutes of the previous light bulb replacement, and one to complain that this wasn't the way they USED to screw in light bulbs.

Q: How many Masons
   does it take to change a light bulb?

A: Twenty, as follows:

Two to complain that the light doesn't work.
        One to pass the problem to the
Master of the Lodge.
    Three to do a study on light in the Lodge.
Two to check out the types of lights the
    Knights of Columbus use.
Five to plan a fund-raising dinner to raise
            money for the replacement bulb.
Three to argue over it.
        Two to complain that 'It's not the way
    we did it before.'
One to borrow a ladder, donate the bulb
            and install it.
One to order the brass 'light bulb
        memorial plate' and have it inscribed.

Q: How many Freemasons
    does it take to change
a light bulb?

A: Three and a chair.

You need one Worshipful Master
            and two Wardens.
    The Worshipful Master
stands on the chair, puts the
        light bulb in the socket
and the wardens turn the chair
            to help him screw it in.

Q: How many Past
      Masters does
it take to change
      a light bulb?

A: Change it?

      Why?

A newly made Freemason is sitting at the festive board talking to the Worshipful Master. The Worshipful Master asks him if he understands what all the Lodge Officers' jobs are.

The newly made Mason responds: 'Well, I know what your job is and I understand what the two men sitting in the other seats did. I can understand why the man on the outside and inside work together to guard the door. However, I have one question.

'Who was that nasty rude man who walked around with me and kept interrupting all the time?'

'That would be the Junior Deacon,' said the Worshipful Master.

Q: Why was King
Solomon
so wise?

A: Because he
had 500 wives
to tell him
what to do!

A Tyler salutes with
his sword.

One Brother said:
'You missed me!'
'Just wait until
you nod,'
said the Tyler.

Some people think
that Masonic
ritual is a matter
of life and death.

I can assure you
it's far more
important
than that!

A young Mason to the
        Director of Ceremonies:
'What do you get for
            becoming Master
    of a Lodge?'

DC: 'A Past Master's apron,
        a Past Master jewel and
an extra five inches on your
            waist measurement.'

(Those who have been there
        will understand.)

A group of Masons are sitting around the festive board. One pipes up, saying: 'I once visited a Lodge in Yorkshire that all wore tricorn hats.'

'That's nothing,' says another Brother, 'I visited a Lodge in Cambridge that all wore

special Masonic suits.'

'I can beat that,' said one old Brother. 'I visited a military Masonic Lodge that met in a submarine. The Tyler had to wear a frog suit.'

Once upon a time an English Mason was visiting a Masonic Lodge in China. However, he didn't know any Chinese, so he was understandably worried when he was asked to do the response on behalf of the guests.

'What shall I do?' he asked his English-speaking host.

'Just stand up, bow to the Worshipful Master, bow to the Senior Warden and then the Junior Warden,' answered his host.

So he stood up, bowed to the Worshipful Master, bowed to the Senior Warden and then bowed to the Junior Warden. The response was a thunderous applause. So he did it again!

He bowed to the Worshipful Master, bowed to the Senior Warden and then bowed to the Junior Warden.

This time everyone booed.

'What did I do wrong?' he asked upon sitting down.

'You went on too long,' said his host.

Q: What do you
   call a porcupine
with an
   apron on?

A: Ma-Sonic
   the Hedgehog!

A gentleman is walking his dog
through his local park when
he notices a rather frantic and
disorganised football match taking
place on the park's football pitch.
'What's going on?'
he asks a spectator who is
watching from the sidelines.
The other replies: 'It's a match
between the Masons and the
Odd Fellows.'
'What's the score?'
asks the first man.
'I don't know,' says the spectator,
'it's a secret.'

'To do
is to be.'—
Plato
'To be
is to do.'—
Kant
'Do be
do be do.'—
Sinatra

One day a Lodge Secretary received a rather worrying phone call from the wife of a newly initiated Brother.

'I don't know what's wrong with him,' she complained. 'He has started behaving very strangely since joining Masonry.'

'In what way?' enquired the Secretary.

'Well,' said the wife, 'he locks himself in the bathroom for hours on end, mumbling to himself with his strange little blue book.'

'Don't worry, I'll have a word with him,' the Secretary replied in a reassuring manner.

Later that evening at the festive board the Secretary had a chance for a quiet word with the Brother in question.

'I understand that you need to learn your lines but why do you have to do it in there?' he asked.

'Well,' said the newly made Brother. 'It's the only TYLED room in the house . . .'

During one particularly hot English summer evening, in the baking heat a Lodge had a bit of bad luck. It was preparing to initiate a candidate and the air conditioner had stopped working. After sweating their way through part of the ritual, the Master asked the candidate: '. . . having been kept in a state of darkness, what, in your present situation, is the predominant wish in your heart?'

The candidate replied: 'A beer.'

At this juncture the WM, being startled, whispered 'light', to the candidate.

'OK,' the candidate replied, 'a lite beer.'

The Worshipful Master of a Lodge is woken in the night by drunken singing in the street outside his house. As he rises to give the singer a piece of his mind, he realises he recognises the voice as that of the Lodge Junior Deacon. So he leans out of his bedroom and sure enough he sees the Junior Deacon staggering down the street in a drunken manner.

'Brother! Where are you going at this time of night in that state?' he demands.

'II'mm on mmyy waayyy . . . to a lecttttuurre . . . on Ffreemmassonnrrry,' replies the JD.

The WM is puzzled and says: 'I can tell by the state of you that you have been to a Lodge meeting already. Where can you possibly get a lecture on Freemasonry at this time of night?'

JD: 'Frromm mmyy wifffe, wwhenn I gget homme!'

On the night of his initiation, one poor Candidate got into his car to drive to the temple, when the car broke down. Not having time to fix the car or even identify the problem, the candidate decided to ride to Lodge on his bicycle.

His bad luck continuing, halfway through the journey, at the top of a large hill, his chain broke! As the Lodge was at the bottom of the other side of the hill all he needed was the back-pedal brake, so he repaired the chain with a cord he had in his pocket and freewheeled downhill to the Lodge.

Later that evening, in reply to a toast in his honour, he said how proud he was to be a Freemason but could not understand, as he had not told anyone, how the WM knew that he had come on his own free wheel and a cord.

Bro Andrew and Bro Mike are in the robing room getting ready for a Lodge meeting. When Andrew opens his case to take out his apron, Mike notices a pair of silk stockings neatly rolled up in the corner of the case.

Mike asks: 'Andrew, what's this with the ladies clothing in your case?'

Andrew gives a sideways glance and whispers: 'You remember the installation meeting last year?'

Mike acknowledges and Andrew goes on: 'Keep it to yourself, but on the way home I stopped off at a pub where I met a beautiful lady. Apparently, she lost her stockings in my car and my wife found them. I told my wife I was passed to a higher degree and, ever since, she takes them out of the case, washes them and puts them back in with my gloves!'

David and Derek had been members of the same Lodge for many years. They promised each other that the first of them to pass to the Grand Lodge above would return to tell the other whether there really was Freemasonry in Heaven, and if so what it was like. By and by, as fate would have it, it was Derek who went first.

One day, on his way to Lodge, David heard a whispering voice from the ether. 'David! It's me!' He looked around but saw nothing.

A few moments later he heard the same voice again, now quite clearly: 'David! It's me, Derek!'

'Derek!' David exclaimed. 'Are you in Heaven?'

'Yes I am,' said Derek.

David took a few moments to regain his composure. 'Well, Derek, are there Lodges up there in Heaven?'

'There certainly are, David. Wonderful Lodges everywhere and they are quite magnificent, far better than anything in Great Queen Street.

The meetings are well attended, the ritual is word perfect, the festive board fantastic, the spirit of Freemasonry is all-pervasive and everyone gets on.'

'My goodness, Derek,' said David. 'It certainly sounds very impressive. Tell me, are you having a good time?'

'Well, David, I have some good news and some bad.'

'OK, so what's the good news?'

'The good news is that we are doing a Third this Thursday.'

'Great,' said David. 'What's the bad news, then?'

'I just got the summons through and you're the Senior Deacon!'

An elderly Mason who passed away, went to Heaven and met with St Peter. He identified himself as a Freemason to St Peter, who asked him: 'What Lodge?' 'Cabbell Lodge, Number 807.' He answered proudly.

'Well,' said St. Peter, 'this might be of interest to you.' He took the Mason to a Heavenly Lodge room. Inside, the never-ending walls were filled with clocks. Each clock had a Lodge's name on a brass plate below it and each clock showed a different time. The Mason asked why and St Peter informed him that the hands moved only when someone in that Lodge made a mistake in the Ritual.

After looking for a while, the man asked: 'Why can't I see the clock for my Lodge?'

St Peter replied: 'Why, it's in the kitchen, of course.'

'The kitchen?' said the Mason.

'Yes,' smiled St Peter, 'you see, we needed a new fan.'

After his initiation a newly made Mason returns home. As I am sure you can imagine, his wife is naturally curious to know what happened. The conversation goes something like this:

She: 'Well, how'd it go?'

He: 'Very well — very interesting.'

She: 'What happened?'

He: 'I can't really tell you about it.'

She: 'Well, is there anything you *can* tell me?'

He: 'Well it seems there are three types of men in the Lodge — walkers, talkers and holy men.'

She: 'What do they do — if you can tell me?'

He: 'The walkers walked me around the Lodge. The talkers talked to me and to the walkers as I was led around . . .'

She: '. . . and the holy men? What of them?'

He: 'They seem to be a special class of men — all in dark blue aprons. They just sit on the benches around the Lodge with their heads in their hands, chanting repeatedly: "Oh My God! Oh My God!"'

A group of police officers decided to boost their success rate of apprehending drink drivers by staking out the local Masonic Hall.

They waited expectantly as the meeting came to the end. The first Mason slowly wobbled down the stairs as drunk as a skunk! He fumbled with his keys for a while and got into his car. As he drove away his car swerved from one side of the road to the other.

As soon as the police officers saw this, they gave chase. Upon stopping the Masonic driver, the two officers asked him to blow into the breathalyser bag. Which he did. To the amazement of the officers, the test proved negative.

Fearing a faulty test they tried again — with the same results. Sure of a possible conviction they then escorted him to the police station for a blood test, with it also proving negative.

Confused, the officers asked the Mason what was going on, to which he answered:

'I had a lovely evening tonight. The Provincial Grand Master was there, the Provincial Grand Secretary was there, the Provincial Grand Stewards were there.'

Still confused, the officers asked him his identity. To which he replied: 'Oh! I'm the Provincial Grand Decoy!'

J ust before a Lodge is about to open, an ancient-looking man approaches the Tyler. 'Ready,' he says. 'What for?' says the Tyler. 'I'm ready to be passed to the Second Degree.'

A complete silence emanates as all the assembled Masons just stare at the old man in confusion.

'I was initiated on December the 12th, 1913. Now I'm ready for my Second Degree.'

So the Secretary looks through the records only to find that the elderly man is telling the truth.

'Where have you been all these years? What took you so long to be ready for your Passing?' they ask.

He replied: 'As it said in the ritual, I was learning to subdue my passions!'

A dedicated Freemason came
     under fire at home one day
  after he had been visiting
       too many Lodges.
His wife said to him:
     'All those masters-in-office
  have to do is click their
fingers and you would be there,
wouldn't you? . . .
     I wish I was a Master!'
'So do I, dear,' he retorted.
    'We swap those every year!'

A man convicted of murder was about to be hanged. The hangman asked the man if he had any last words before he was executed. 'Yes,' said the man, 'I hate Freemasons!'

'Why do you hate Freemasons?' the hangman asked.

'The man I murdered was a Freemason,' explained the murderer. 'The sheriff who found me out and arrested me was a Freemason, the Prosecutor who tried my case was a Freemason and the Judge who presided at the trial was a Freemason. I also suspect many of the jury who found me guilty and sentenced me to death were Freemasons!'

'Is that all you have to say?' asked the hangman, 'Yes,' replied the killer.

'Then you will advance one step with your left foot.'

Tony and Terry were on their way home from a Rose Croix meeting. Tony was giving Terry a lift. He shouldn't have been driving, however, because he was a bit tipsy.

When the traffic cop pulled them over they hoped that he would be a Mason and let them off!

'Racing home are we, sir?' said the policeman. 'Michael Schumacher are we sir?'

At this point Terry noticed that the policeman was wearing a square and compasses lapel pin. Terry whispered to Tony:

'He doesn't know you're a Mason! Show him your cross!'

Tony shouted: 'Why don't you piss off and leave us alone?'

One day, whilst walking past a Masonic regalia shop, one of two friends noticed an advert in the window: 'Masonic Parrots for Sale.'

Curiosity made them enter the shop and enquire: 'What is this Masonic Parrot advert all about?'

The shopkeeper immediately showed them through to the back room where, on a tall perch, was a parrot, light blue in colour. 'That's a Master Parrot. He can recite all Three Degrees word perfectly,' he said.

'How much?' they asked. '£10,000,' the shopkeeper replied.

'That's a lot of money,' the first friend retorted. 'Have you any other parrots?'

'Yes,' said the shopkeeper. He went in the back and returned with a magnificent dark blue parrot. 'This is a Provincial Grand Parrot,' he said. 'It can recite all Three Degrees and all the addresses in the back of the book, that no one ever looks at, word perfect, He will cost you £25.'

'Blimey!' said the friend. 'Have you anything cheaper?'

The shopkeeper disappeared again and returned with a slightly scruffy old bird in dark blue but with gold braid down its wings and tail. 'This is a Grand Parrot,' he said. 'He is only ten quid.'

'What does he do?' the men asked.

'Nothing. He just sits there shaking his head and going "Tut, tut . . . tut, tut".'

One evening after a particularly *festive*, festive board, one Brother had partaken of too much wine. The Worshipful Master was very worried. He did not want the Brother to drive home in his present state of intoxication as he lived some distance away. So he insisted that the Brother stay the night at his house and travel home the next morning. After much persuasion, this is what he did.

When he got home the next morning, his wife was furious with him because he had forgotten to phone. She did not believe his story about staying with a Brother because of the state he had been in, but was worried he had been with another woman. However, she pretended to believe him by asking how the ceremony had gone, how many other Brethren had been there and all the regular questions that wives ask. So he told her that it had been an excellent Lodge meeting and that 55 Brethren had attended.

At the next Lodge meeting, when the Secretary rose to read out correspondence, he read a letter from the wife asking if the Brother, with whom her husband had stayed the night after the last Lodge meeting, would please write to her and confirm his story.

The next day she received 54 letters in the post.

A newly made Worshipful Master was walking along at the seaside when he found a bottle with a Genie in it. 'I am the genie of the bottle and I will grant you one wish,' said the Genie.

'Not three wishes?' said the WM.

'No, just the one,' said the Genie.

'OK,' thought the newly made Master, 'I will wish for something that is of benefit both to myself and Freemasonry in general. Something that benefits us all.'

So he says to the Genie: 'I've always wanted to go to America to see how Freemasonry is done there but I am scared to fly. So my wish is for you to build a bridge between Britain and America. That way both English and American Masons can drive over and visit each other whenever they like!'

'What?' exclaimed the Genie. 'How can you expect me to do that? Think of the materials that would be needed! Do you know how deep the water is in that ocean? Have you thought how far it is? Don't you know that's impossible? No one could do that, not even a Genie. You will have to make another wish.'

'OK,' said the Master. 'I wish that throughout the world Freemasonry works how it should. I wish that all the Freemasons get on and that the Past Masters stop "tutting" and criticising. I wish that the rituals all go well and that the candidates learn from the rituals and apply the meanings and lessons to their lives. I wish that every festive board is fun and that everybody's speeches are short and to the point.'

'Hmmmmm,' said the Genie after some thought. 'Do you want that bridge with two lanes or four?'

One poor Brother is driving home from Lodge through central London and finds himself in desperate need to urinate. He looks everywhere for a place to park but every street is covered in double yellow lines. Eventually he gives up and parks on the double yellows next to a public toilet. Needless to say, as soon as he parks a traffic warden appears.

Hoping the traffic warden is a Bro, the Mason pulls out his driving licence and puts it in his ritual book and hands it to the traffic warden, who fails to bat an eyelid.

'Officer,' he says, 'if you don't mind I am going to park here just for a second or two. I must just restore myself to my personal comforts.'

'Right you are, Sir,' said the traffic warden, 'and on your return, I shall call your attention to a Charge.'

Boy to Mum:
'Mum, how do
buffaloes make
love?'

Mum:
'I don't know,
ask your Dad.
He's a Mason.'

A newly Raised Brother is discussing his membership with a Proposer. He tells him that, though he's really enjoying his Masonry, it is causing problems with his wife. 'When I come home from a Lodge meeting, I try to be very quiet. I close the front door carefully behind me, lock it with the utmost stealth, take off my shoes and tiptoe upstairs. I get undressed in the dark, pee quietly and don't flush the loo. However, whatever I do, my wife wakes up and is very angry that her sleep has been disturbed. Then we go into a large argument about what time I get in from Lodge, 'I have the solution,' says the more experienced Brother. 'Do the opposite. Come in loudly, slam the door, stomp upstairs, and shout "I'm home dear and I'm in the mood for some sexy loving!"

'I absolutely guarantee she'll be fast asleep before you reach the bedroom.'

Recently an English Lodge had a visit from a French Lodge and after the Lodge proceedings they all retired to the festive board. The French Director of Ceremonies was seated next to the English DC and conversation about all things ensued. The English DC was particularly impressed by the well-spoken English of the French Brother and decided that he should at least attempt some conversation in the other's tongue.

Just then a fly alighted on the table and the English DC, pointing to the fly, remarked: 'Regarde le mouche!'

'Ah!' said our continental Brother, 'LA mouche, the fly is female.' At the next Lodge Committee Meeting the DC summing up the visitation said: 'Well, I was particularly taken by the French DC's command of English, but what impressed me even more was his fantastic eyesight!'

While paying a visit to North Wales, I was about five hours too early for the meeting. Going into the local pub, which was next door to the Masonic Hall, I was invited to take one of their guide dogs, which would lead me on a tour of the local beauty spots.

Of the three presented I chose the DC dog, which was reputed to know everywhere and everything.

And he certainly did — he was absolutely excellent.

Upon revisiting the area, many months later, I took advantage of the same offer, but couldn't have the same dog, as the owner explained that since my last visit the DC dog had received Honours, and therefore did not go out on guide trips.

I asked: 'What does he do now then?'

'Oh, he just sits on his arse and barks!' was the reply.

At the monthly Masonic Building Society meeting much discussion raged about the problem of mice in the Lodge building. Of course several suggestions on how to be rid of them were offered — set mouse traps; lay mouse poison; call an exterminator; buy a cat etc. The building manager took all this advice under consideration and it was agreed that at the next meeting he would make a report on his progress. Sure enough, at the next meeting he was questioned. 'Did you use my idea of a cat?' 'Did you use poison or traps?' Finally, he said: 'All the mice are gone.' Everyone wanted to know how he had accomplished such a feat.

'Well . . .' he said, 'I initiated all the mice into my Lodge and I haven't seen one attend since!'

A team of archaeologists were excavating in Israel when they came upon a cave. Written across the wall of the cave were some curious symbols. It was considered a unique find and the writings were said to be at least three thousand years old! The piece of stone was removed, brought to the museum, and archaeologists from around the world came to study the ancient symbols.

They held a huge meeting after months of conferences to discuss the meaning of the markings. The President of the society pointed at the first drawing and said: 'This looks like a woman. We can judge that it was family oriented and held women in high esteem. You can also tell they were intelligent, as the next symbol resembles a donkey, so they were smart enough to have animals help them till the soil. The next drawing looks like a shovel of some sort, which means they even had tools to help them. Even further proof of their high intelligence is the fish, which means that if a famine had hit the earth, whereby the food didn't grow, they would take to the sea for food. The last symbol appears to be the Star of David which means they were evidently Hebrews.'

The audience applauded enthusiastically, but a little old man stood up at the back of the room and said: 'Idiots, Hebrew is read from right to left. It says: "Holy Mackerel, Dig the Ass on that Woman!"'

There once was an American who decided to write a book about famous Masonic Lodges around the world. For his first chapter he decided to write about English Lodges. So he booked his tickets and finally arrived in Liverpool, thinking that he would work his way across the country from west to east.

On his first day he was inside a Lodge taking photographs, when he noticed a golden telephone mounted on the wall with a sign that read '£10,000 per call'. The American, being intrigued, asked a Brother who was strolling by what the telephone was used for. The Brother replied that it was a direct line to Heaven and that for £10,000 you could talk to the Great Architect. The American thanked the Brother and went along his way.

The American's next stop was in Manchester. There, while at a very large Masonic Centre, he saw the same golden telephone with the same sign under it. He wondered if this was the same kind of telephone he saw in Liverpool and he asked a nearby Brother what its purpose was. The Brother told him that it was a direct line to Heaven and that for £10,000 he could talk to the Great Architect. 'OK, thank you,' said the American.

The American travelled on to Leeds, Birmingham, Leicester and many other places. At every Lodge he stopped at he saw the same golden telephone with the same '£10,000 per call' sign under it, and every time the American asked a member of the Lodge what the phone was for he got the same answer — 'It's a direct line to Heaven and for £10,000 you can talk to the Great Architect.'

Finally, the American arrived at Great Queen Street and again he saw the same golden telephone but this time the sign under it read '10p per call'. The American was intrigued and he told a Grand Officer: 'Most Worshipful Brother, I have travelled all over England and I have seen this same golden telephone in many Lodges. I have found out that it is a direct line to Heaven, but in all the other cities the cost to call Heaven was £10,000. Why is it so cheap here?'

The Most Worshipful Brother smiled and answered: 'You are in London now, son. It's a local call.'

A wife heard her husband
    come back into the house
not too long after he had left
    for the night.
    She said:
'Honey, I thought you were
going to your Lodge meeting.'
'It was postponed.' He replied.
    'The wife of the
Generalissimo Grand
    Exalted Invincible
Supreme Potentate wouldn't
    let him attend tonight.'

I was asked, at the last minute, to
          reply on behalf of the guests.
After the usual polite niceties, I then
          informed the assembled Brethren
that the six men on the top table were
          my biological brothers.
The first was an accountant and the
                second knew nothing about
figures either,
          the third was a copper and the
fourth occupied the cell next to him,
     the fifth was a financial advisor, and
the sixth was also a rogue,
          and me, the seventh, well I am
a bachelor, just like our father.

While acting as IG, I asked our
    candidate if he felt anything.
Being a true Scotsman, he replied:
    'A wee prick.' Our JD, realising
his mistake, leaned over and
whispered: 'I do.'
        Later, at festive board, I rose to
congratulate him but also stated I had
    a concern about his hearing.
'When I greeted you at the door of the
        Lodge I asked you
            if you felt anything . . .
                not who you were with!'

Two Master Masons were enjoying a flight in a hot air balloon when suddenly a thick cloud formed between them and the ground. Being without instruments, after an hour they realised that they were well and truly lost. A short time later they came across a large hole in the cloud and espied a gentleman below walking his dog across a field. They had time to exchange pleasantries and found that he too was a member of the Craft. The chaps in the balloon enquired of him as to their location and received the reply: 'About 200 feet up in a balloon.'

Just then the cloud closed the hole and they were alone again. One turned to the other and said: 'I bet he's the Secretary of his Lodge!'

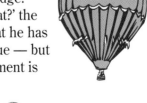

'Why do you say that?' the other asked. 'Well, what he has told us is absolutely true — but in our present predicament is totally useless!'

Worshipful Master:

   'Brother Senior Warden,
the labours of the evening
   being ended, you have my
command to close the Lodge.'

Senior Warden:

'Worshipful Master, Brethren,
      in the name of . . .
(mumbles and looks
      confused) . . . Good God!
What's his name again . . ?'

Most Masons are very
law-abiding but some
of them get mixed
up when it comes to the
difference between
the amount of alcohol
you can take through
Customs and the
amount you are
allowed to drink
and drive.

I was talking to Martin and
Josh about joining their
Lodge. Josh said there were
two types of member:
'I'm a Full Member,
and Martin's a
Country Member.'
'Yes,' I said. 'I remember,
but you speak that
way of your Brothers?'

A young Entered Apprentice was being tested on his memory and proficiency.

After displaying the signs and passwords he had learned, he asked: 'I have noticed several of the older members sticking their fingers in their ears and whistling. What does that sign mean?' 'That's not a sign,' replied the DC. 'That's just the Past Masters adjusting their hearing aids.'

A Masonic postman, doing his rounds, picked up a letter from a postbox that was addressed to 'God'. The postman, seeing that the letter was not sealed and had no stamp on it, opened it and read it. It was from a man who was down on his luck and was asking God for help. The letter asked for £50 to get his family through the next week.

The postman, being a Mason, took the letter to Lodge that evening, read it, and asked for donations for the unfortunate fellow. The Masons, wanting to help, took a collection, and received £25 from the Brethren. The Secretary placed the cash in a Lodge envelope, and gave it to the postman to deliver the following day, which he did.

Another day passed and the postman again found an unsealed letter in the post box addressed to 'God'. Again he opened and read the letter, which thanked God for the money but instructed him to send it through the Odd Fellows next time, as the Masons had kept half of what had been sent last time.

Knock! Knock! Knock!

'Who's there?'

Knock! Knock! Knock!

'Who's there?!'

'Hang on!

Don't you mean —

whom have you there?'

A tired old Mason
      whose hair was grey,
Came to the gates
         of Heaven one day.
When asked what, on Earth,
      he had done the most,
He said he had replied to the
      Visitor's Toast.
St Peter said,
      as he tolled the bell,
'Come inside my Brother,
      you've had enough
         of Hell.'

I
always thought
a Freemason
was a man
who builds
houses
for nothing.

Masonic Survival Kit

Always make sure that the following items are in your regalia case whenever you attend a meeting:

Toothpick
Rubber Band
A Plaster
Pencil
Eraser
Chewing Gum
Mint
Tea Bag

Why these items?

1. TOOTHPICK
To remind you to pick out the good qualities in others
Matt. 7:1

2. RUBBER BAND
To remind you to be flexible; things might not always go the way you want, but it will work out
Romans 8:28

3. A PLASTER
To remind you to heal hurt feelings,
yours or someone else's
Col. 3:12-14

4. PENCIL
To remind you to list your blessings everyday
Eph. 1:3

5. ERASER
To remind you that everyone makes mistakes,
and it's OK
Gen. 50:15-21

6. CHEWING GUM
To remind you to stick with it
and you can accomplish anything
Phil. 4:13

7. MINT
To remind you that you are worth a mint!
John 3:16-17

8. TEA BAG
To remind you to relax daily
and go over that list of blessings
1 Thess. 5:18

A recently raised Master Mason applied for a job and, knowing his prospective boss to be a prominent Mason, he made sure to wear his square and compass cuff links. When he arrived at the interview he approached his interviewer in the regular manner and proceeded to shake hands (yes, with THAT handshake).

After an hour or so (with the candidate dropping numerous Masonic references) the prospective boss asked, if he were to be offered the job, what package would he expect. Our candidate, now feeling very confident, said that he would like £20,000 and five weeks of annual leave.

His interviewer replied: 'We'll halve it and you begin.'

I was once a visitor at a Lodge and was
introduced to the Tate family.

First there was the old man WM DIC-TATE, who
wants to run everything his way, and his cousin
WBro RO-TATE who wants to change
everything.
Brother AGI-TATE stirs up trouble
with his nephew Bro IRRI-TATE.
When new ideas are suggested
Bro HESI-TATE and his son VEGE-TATE
both want to leave them until next year.
Brother IMI-TATE wants everything
to be like it was in his Mother Lodge.
Brother DEVAS-TATE is a voice of doom —
but Brother FACILI-TATE is most helpful.
Brother COGI-TATE and Brother MEDI-TATE
think things over carefully — but poor old
Brother AMPU-TATE has cut himself
off completely.

Have you heard the story about that Mason who wanted to go hunting? He needed a dog and consulted a Brother. That Brother, who sold dogs, gave him one, called JW.

'It's a very good dog,' he said. 'He knows a lot about hunting and you can truly rely on him.'

Our fellow took that dog. One week later, he returned. 'It's not too bad, but he doesn't seem to be very experienced. Haven't you got another dog?'

'Sure I have,' said the Brother. 'This one, for example, is called SW and he's a bit more experienced. Try him and if you don't like him, feel free to come back.'

Indeed, our fellow returned the dog two weeks later. 'He's quite good actually, but he's not what I'm looking for. Still I need a dog which is more experienced.'

'Well,' said the Brother, 'I can offer you a really experienced dog. He's called PM and you'll have good time with him.'

So, our fellow took the animal. Just one day later, he returned.

'What's wrong with him?' the Brother asked. 'I haven't got another dog that is more experienced than this one.'

'Well,' our fellow said, 'he might be experienced, but all he's doing is sitting there and barking!'

A Freemason is on a day trip to a small village somewhere in the north of England. He finds himself wondering if there is a Masonic Lodge there. So he takes a walk through the village and by luck he finds a path called 'Mason's Road'. 'This path must lead to the local Masonic temple,' he thinks. So he follows it. At the end of the pathway, he sees a building, which looks somewhat rundown and in disuse. Our Brother tries to open the door and finds it is unlocked. He goes inside and finds dust and spider webs everywhere. In front of a door there sits a skeleton, wearing an apron and a collar, and holding a sword in its hand. 'O my God!' thinks our Brother and enters the Lodge room. In puzzlement, he sees skeletons with collars and aprons everywhere. The WM, the Wardens, the Organist, Deacons — all skeletons. He looks around and goes to the seats of the Secretary and Treasurer.

Under the hand of the Treasurer, he finds a small piece of paper, a little note, which he seems to have passed to the Secretary. So our Brother picks up the note, blows away the dust and reads: 'If nobody prompts the WM, we will sit here for ever!'

Masonry goes back
   to the days of King Arthur's court.
King Arthur called a Lodge meeting
   in the castle at sundown.
         Launcelot was out in the
town meeting with a lot of friends
   (ie Guinevere) and forgot the time.
On hearing the horn announce
sundown, he immediately said
                 goodbye and
   raced back on his horse to get back
to the castle in time.
         However, the drawbridge was
just being raised. He raced and
         jumped . . . but too late.
   As he fell he said: 'So moat it be.'

A Candidate for Initiation in a
        country Lodge had been
teased at length about
        what was going to
happen to him.

        Unfortunately, one Brother
attending came straight from
        market where he had
        bought a goat, which was
tethered outside.
    The Candidate
arrived, saw the goat
    and fled, never to
be seen again.

Fred was eager to progress and
    never turned down a request,
even at short notice.

        Some started to take
advantage of him until one
    morning he was having a lie-in
when the telephone went at
        7:30am. Before he could
speak, he was asked to attend a
    10am meeting, nearly two
hours' drive away. He passed it to
    his wife, saying, loudly
enough to be heard on the phone:
        'Darling! I think someone
wants your husband.'

The Grand Master, Grand Secretary and Grand Treasurer are walking to lunch when they find an antique oil lamp. They rub it and a Genie comes out in a puff of smoke.

The Genie says: 'I usually grant only three wishes, so I'll give each of you just one.'

'Me first! Me first!' says Grand Treasurer. 'I want to be in the Bahamas, driving a speedboat, without a care in the world.' Poof! He's gone. 'Me next! Me next!' says Grand Secretary in astonishment. 'I want to be in Hawaii, relaxing on the beach with my personal masseuse, an endless supply of pina coladas and the love of my life.' Poof! He's gone. 'OK, you're up,' the Genie says to the Grand Master.

The Grand Master says: 'I want those two back in the office after lunch'.

Moral of this story:
Always let your Grand Master
have the first say.

72

Once upon a time there was a Lodge located in the backwoods of rural England, where the Brethren were all faithful Masons but lacked the knowledge of receiving Brothers from other jurisdictions. During one of the meetings the Junior Deacon informs the Worshipful Master that there is an alarm at the door, whereupon the WM replies: 'Attend the alarm and report your findings.' The Junior Deacon opens the door and sees to his amazement a Brother impeccably dressed with an elaborate apron and jewels about his chest.

The Tyler being somewhat slow to answer for the visiting Brother, the visitor states: 'My name is John Smith, PM of my Lodge, Past District Deputy Grand Master of my district, Past Grand Master of My Grand Lodge, who humbly requests an audience with the Worshipful Master.'

The Junior Deacon, upon hearing those words from the visitor and seeing the elaborate apron and jewels upon his chest, immediately closes the door, returns to his post and informs the Worshipful Master: 'Worshipful Master, The Grand Architect of the Universe is at the door!'

They say
Freemasonry is
universal but . . .

. . . If an Ephramite
applied to join,
would he be able to
progress beyond
the First Degree?

One doddery old Secretary, well past
    his sell-by date, delivers the Second
Degree tracing board to the Lodge.
        Though his effort is admirable,
the performance is really very slow.
        The Brethren all have respect for
him due to his age and his Grand
        Rank, but really what should
have been completed in 20 minutes
    takes almost double that time.
Once the presentation is over the
    Master speaks, thanking him for his
effort on behalf of the Lodge, and asks
        him to write letters of condolence
to the families of the Forty and
      Two Thousand Ephramites
          reported slain
           during the presentation!

During the car journey home from a Masonic meeting on a dark stormy night, a Mason loses it on a corner, ending up quite safe but stuck in a ditch. He staggers up to the road and the first set of headlights that come along are those of a tractor driven by a farmer. He stops and willingly tows him out of the ditch and insists he follow him to his farm just down the road, where he is offered overnight accommodation, the use of the telephone and a bath. In the morning his clothes have been cleaned and pressed and a hearty breakfast is provided. In thanking the farmer they shake hands and the Mason realises that the farmer is a Brother. 'Well, there you go,' he says, 'I suppose you did all that because you realised I was on the Square by my black tie and Masonic bag in the car etc.' The farmer smiles and replies: 'No my friend, I did it not because you are a Mason but rather that I am!'

One poor Mason whose
mind was on the festive
board ended the meeting
with: 'All that is left is for
us to lock up our secrets
in the sacred suppository'!
The Brethren of the
Lodge united in the act of
laughing loud in
response to this one!

A Freemason parks his brand-new Porsche in front of the Lodge to show it off to his Brethren. As he's getting out of the car, a lorry comes speeding along too close to the kerb and takes off the door before speeding off.

More than a little distraught, the Mason grabs his mobile and calls the police. Five minutes later, the police arrive. He starts screaming hysterically:

'My Porsche, my beautiful red Porsche is ruined. No matter how long it takes at the panel beaters, it'll simply never be the same again!' After the Brother finally finishes his rant, the policeman shakes his head in disgust: 'I can't believe how materialistic you bl**dy Masons are. You lot are so focused on your possessions that you don't notice anything else in your life.'

'How can you say such a thing at a time like this?' snaps the Brother. The policeman replies: 'Didn't you realise that your right arm was torn off when the lorry hit you?'

The Brother looks down in absolute horror: 'BL**DY HELL!!!!!!', he screams . . . 'Where's my Rolex ???? . . .'

Did you hear the one
    about the poor candidate
for initiation
        who had diarrhoea?

He didn't know whether
            to roll his trouser
leg up, or pull his
            pants down!

Do you know a Masonic joke
that should be included in
the next edition of

*How Many Freemasons
Does it Take to Change a Light Bulb?*

Why not email it to us at

jokes@lewismasonic.com